Welcome to Zairy Designs!

My name is Linda, and I've created these mandalas and patterns to incorporate Celtic knot-work and traditional hand-engraving designs with a stained glass aesthetic.

I hope that you will enjoy them.

Please find my page on Facebook at
https://www.facebook.com/Zairy-Designs

ISBN-13:
978-0692141694 (Zairy)

ISBN-10:
0692141693

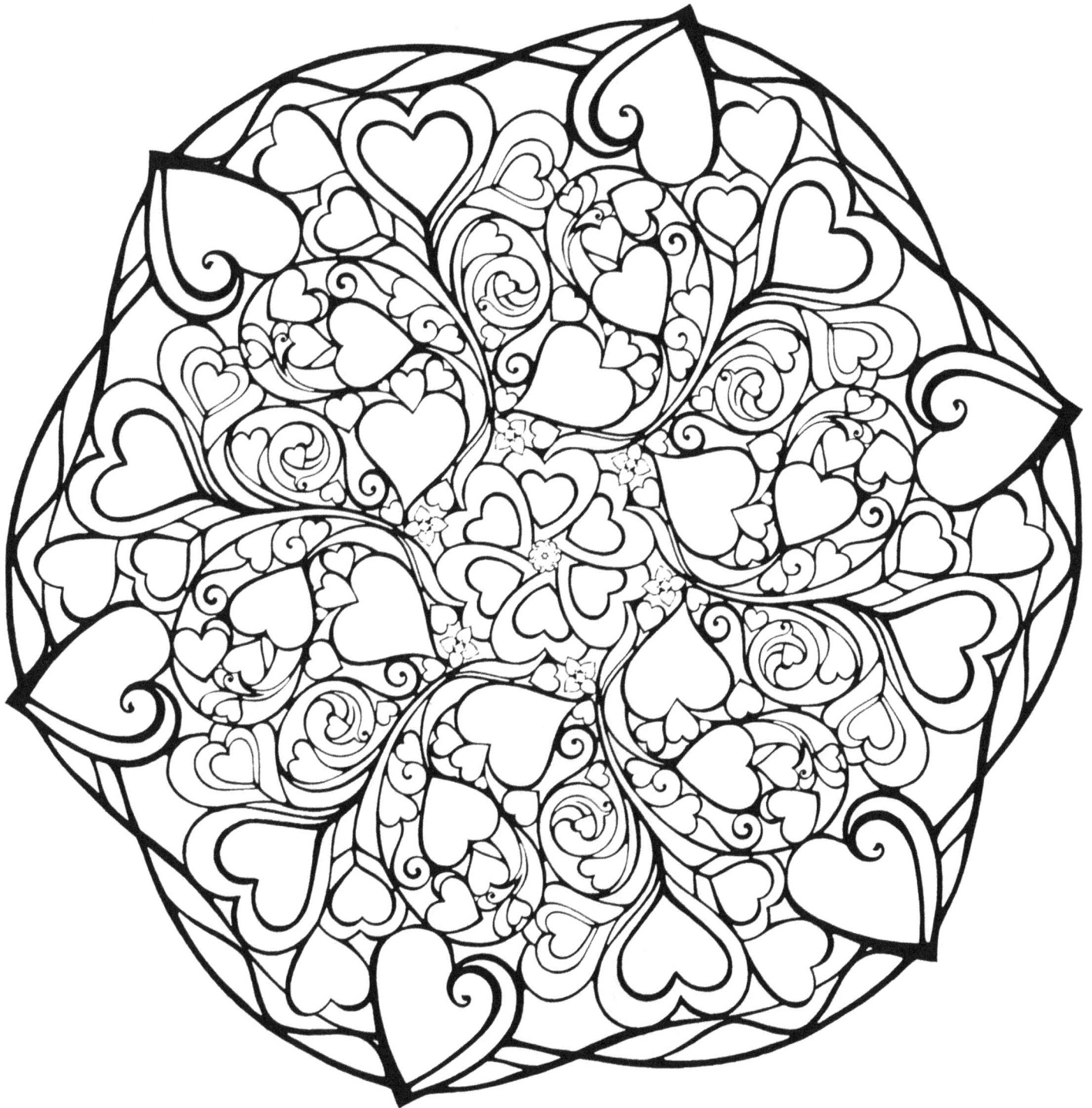

ACKNOWLEDGEMENTS

I would like to thank CPT Dan Roberts,
without whose encouragement
I would never have created this book.
I am also grateful to my supportive husband,
community of friends,
and the bloggers and 'YouTubers' whose instructions
got me through the process. Mostly...
I thank Amazon for this platform from which to launch.
I do not thank my two dogs, who have been nothing but
distracting and downright obstructive.
I still love them, though.

www.ingramcontent.com/pod-product-compliance
Lightning Source LLC
Chambersburg PA
CBHW080533030426

42337CB00023B/4717